CONTENTS

The Answer _____ Peter Cliffe
The Call _____ C.W. Wade
Grey Eyes _____ Sara Teasdale
No Easy Way _____ Noel Scott
The Laggard _____ Ianthe Jerrold
April Love _____ Peter Cliffe
Spring Song _____ Latimer McInnes
Thoughts From The City _____ Frances Reed
Blue Of The Bluebells _____ Sydney Bell
The Stripling Thames _____ St John Lucas
Spring Rain _____ Sara Teasdale
Breakdown _____ Marion Elliott
Buttercups And Daisies _____ Eileen Melrose
By Carmarthen Bay _____ Wilfrid Gibson
Mixed Brews _____ Clive Sansom
Down The Lane _____ Shan Bullock
Check _____ James Stephens
Canadian Camping Song _____ J.D. Edgar
Plymouth _____ Ernest Radford
Blossomtime _____ Moyra Phyllis Crimp
The Wool Work Picture _____ Aileen E. Passmore
A Song _____ Richard Watson Dixon
Snooze Muse _____ J.M. Robertson
Missed! _____ P.G. Wodehouse
We'll Go No More A-Roving _____ George Gordon, Lord Byron
By The Seashore _____ Latimer McInnes
Ministering Angel _____ Iris Hesselden
Granny's Attic _____ J.M. Robertson
Dorothy _____ Hylda C. Cole
Consolation _____ Shan Bullock
A Wish _____ Tinsley Pratt
Willow Warbler's Song _____ Lilian Maude Watts
Welcome _____ Lord Byron
The Warning _____ Peter Cliffe
The Summerhouse _____ Margaret Ingall
High Summer _____ Kathleen O'Farrell
Fell Walking Song _____ Iris Hesselden
The Cottage _____ John Hogben
Armchair Traveller _____ Iris Hesselden
Suggestion _____ Dorothy Anderson
Spiders _____ Susan O'Mahony
The Shell _____ William Mackay
Roses In The Rain _____ Margaret H. Dixon
Request _____ Iris M. Raikes
River Song _____ Iris Hesselden
A Memory _____ Kathleen O'Farrell
As Winter Comes _____ Sydney Bell
The Visionary _____ Emily Bronte
November _____ Noel Scott
The Pebble _____ Bryan Cave-Browne-Cave

The
Fireside Book

A picture and a poem
for every mood
chosen by

David Hope

Printed and published by
D.C. THOMSON & CO., LTD.,
185 Fleet Street, LONDON EC4A 2HS.
© D. C. Thomson & Co., Ltd., 1994.
ISBN 0-85116-587-7

THE ANSWER

NAKED branches of the chestnut,
   Stark above the rutted lane,
Seem to ask a question mutely:
   When will Springtime come again?

Child beside the window watching
   Slanting shafts of silver rain,
Do you also sadly wonder
   When will Springtime come again?

Lapwings wheeling o'er the ploughland,
   Lately seas of rustling grain,
Fill the air with their lamenting:
   Surely Spring will come again?

Snowdrops in my garden dancing
   Give to me the answer plain.
Earth is resting, dreaming, waiting:
   Spring will soon be here again!

Peter Cliffe

THE CALL

I LONG to smell the clean salt air
  And hear the sea birds scream,
I yearn to feel the vessel's heave
    And the wind as it blows abeam.

The frigate bird and the albatross
    And the petrel call to me,
And the South-east trades in my dreams say "Come
    Once more to the open sea!"

There's life on the sea for the tough he-man
    With red blood in his veins,
For the man whose pulses gladly leap
    When the cordage creaks and strains;

For the man who feels that life is good
    When all the rigging hums.
Ho! list, ye landsmen to the call,
    When the bulging main sheet drums.

For who would sleep o' nights and dream
    In a stuffy room ashore
While the wake of a tall ship foams behind
    And the blue waves stretch before.

So I must answer the call again,
    And down to the sea must go.
Though the foam-flecked crests of the billows toss
    And the stormy tempests blow.

C. W. Wade

GREY EYES

IT was April when you came
  The first time to me,
And my first look in your eyes
  Was like my first look at the sea.

We have been together
  Four Aprils now,
Watching for the green
  On the swaying willow bough;

Yet whenever I turn
  To your grey eyes over me,
It is as though I looked
  For the first time at the sea.

Sara Teasdale

NO EASY WAY

EACH flower, each bush, each plant that grows
  Enchants the eye, delights the nose
With sight and scent. In beds and rows
Their multi-fashioned beauty shows.
The perfume floats; the colour glows . . .
But only through the toil of those
Who ply the spade, the rake, the hoes,
And scare the sparrows, starlings, crows
Who'd steal the seeds the gardener sows.

A garden will its charms disclose —
But not for posturing or pose!
The rich reward's reserved for those
Who love the soil . . . and so dispose
Their time and talents where it shows . . .
A truth that every gardener knows!

Noel Scott

THE LAGGARD

AS down this winding lane I go
　　My ears are quick, my feet are slow,
For "Stop!" the blackthorn cries to me,
And "Stop!" each cloudy sallow-tree.

"Turn, turn again!" the blackthorn cries,
"For wisdom enters at the eyes,
And he that hurries past these snows
He is not wise as folly goes!"

"Stay!" call the sallows, "do not miss
One golden grain the sunbeams kiss!
We fleet, we fade, and when next year
We come, you may not still be here!"

I look and look, and yet again,
Till down both snow and gold-dust rain,
And of that beauty now no more
I have not garnered half the store!

So swift the sun fulfills his days,
So orderly the bough obeys,
That I, who watched the sticky sheaf,
Now linger for the crackling leaf;

And as a-frost I stand and look
And learn the burnt boughs as a book,
There comes a breeze, a drift of rain,
And the burnt boughs are green again!

Old reaper, waiting at some stile,
Bear back your scythe full many a mile!
Or doze, and stay, and give me grace —
I will not mend my laggard's pace!

Ianthe Jerrold

APRIL LOVE

NOW days of Spring are new again,
    And bitter frosts are few again,
'Neath skies turned bright and blue again
I long to be with you again.

Up little hills we'll climb again,
Hear church bells sweetly chime again;
With happiness sublime again,
We'll pay no heed to time again.

We'll stroll beside the rill again,
While nesting birds call shrill again;
I'll know that sudden thrill again,
And say "I love you still" again.

Peter Cliffe

SPRING SONG

THE blackthorn spray is white with may,
   The lark is in the blue;
Throstle and merle, like boy and girl,
   Are mating two and two;
The rooks above, more staid in love,
   Have ceased their noisy strife:
Their wooing past, they know at last
   The cares of wedded life.

You smile to see the silly glee
   Of lambs that scamper by,
Or pause to hear, dulcet and clear,
   The vagrant cuckoo's cry;
The lizard lone, brown as the stone
   Whereon it basking lies,
Touched with your stick, goes darting quick
   In laughable surprise.

Their scent betrays those primrose fays
   Behind their shaggy screen;
Ah, there they shine in troops divine,
   With violets in between;
And 'mid the bloom of furze or broom
   You catch the vacant tune
Of some rash bee that, sallying free,
   Takes April days for June.

And you yourself, you laugh at pelf,
   You shake off cark and care,
The sunshine shoots down to the roots
   Of many an old despair:
And swift as thought, by magic wrought,
   The boughs in blossom swing,
And life renewed, all rosy-hued,
   Puts on the garb of spring!

Latimer McInnes

THOUGHTS FROM THE CITY

MY heart is in the Highlands where the purple
heather blows
And the honeyed air is scented, clear and cool;
My heart it loves the islands where the ocean's tide-
race flows,
And all heaven lies reflected in a pool.

My spirit roams the byways where the grouse and
muircock call
And the peace and beauty heal the troubled soul;
Oh, I shun the city highways where the shallow
pleasures pall
And would let the gifts of Nature make me
whole.

My footsteps walk the woodlands in my thoughts
    and in my dreams,
    Together with the wildcat and the deer;
I see the mountain torrents leap to where the cool
    surf creams
    On the beaches where the sand is white and
    clear.

My happiness is sailing on the Firth's wide sparkling
    breast,
    With my friends who are so staunch, sincere and
    true;
And e'en, my senses failing, I shall find at last my
    rest.
    'Neath that western sky of misty harebell-blue.

Frances Reed

BLUE OF THE BLUEBELLS

IF it's blue you would see you should wander with
me
   Where the Shimna goes winding to Newcastle
   shore;
By her sparkle in Spring you will hear the birds sing
   Of the blue of the bluebells in green Tollymore.

The blue of the sea is a wonder to me,
   At the blue of Slieve Donard my low spirits soar,
But no colour or treat makes my heart miss a beat
   Like the blue of the bluebells in green Tollymore.

The azaleas in bloom are a tonic for gloom
   And the song of the Cascade is balm to the soul;
And the great Sisters Seven lift their branches to
   Heaven
   When by cedar and mountain the thunderclouds
   roll.

From the Hermitage cool you may watch the dark
   pool
   Where a silvery splash brings delight to the eye;
And below the tall trees there's a pine-scented
   breeze
   And the rustle of leaves as old Brock snuffles by.

There are bridges with grace, and of deer there's a
   trace
   Where the proud golden eagle of old used to
   soar;
But my thanks I will give, every Spring that I live,
   For the blue of the bluebells, in green Tollymore.

Sydney Bell

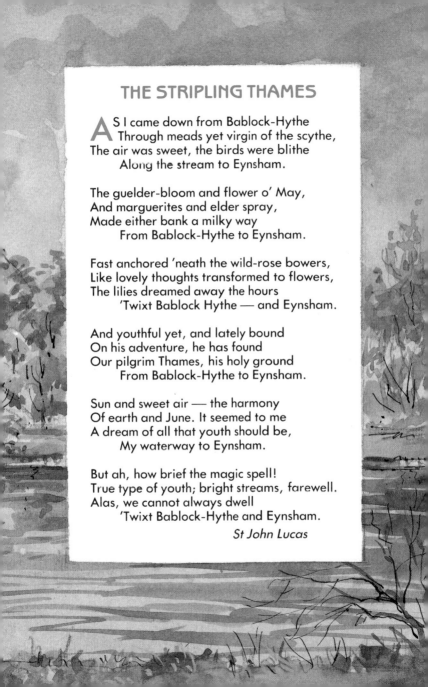

THE STRIPLING THAMES

AS I came down from Bablock-Hythe
Through meads yet virgin of the scythe,
The air was sweet, the birds were blithe
    Along the stream to Eynsham.

The guelder-bloom and flower o' May,
And marguerites and elder spray,
Made either bank a milky way
    From Bablock-Hythe to Eynsham.

Fast anchored 'neath the wild-rose bowers,
Like lovely thoughts transformed to flowers,
The lilies dreamed away the hours
    'Twixt Bablock Hythe — and Eynsham.

And youthful yet, and lately bound
On his adventure, he has found
Our pilgrim Thames, his holy ground
    From Bablock-Hythe to Eynsham.

Sun and sweet air — the harmony
Of earth and June. It seemed to me
A dream of all that youth should be,
    My waterway to Eynsham.

But ah, how brief the magic spell!
True type of youth; bright streams, farewell.
Alas, we cannot always dwell
    'Twixt Bablock-Hythe and Eynsham.

St John Lucas

SPRING RAIN

I THOUGHT I had forgotten,
   But it all came back again
Tonight with the first Spring thunder
   In a rush of rain.

I remembered a darkened doorway
   Where we stood while the storm swept by,
Thunder gripping the earth
   And lightning scrawled on the sky.

The passing motor buses swayed,
   For the street was a river of rain.
Lashed into little golden waves
   In the lamp-light's stain.

With the wild Spring rain and thunder
   My heart was wild and gay;
Your eyes said more to me that night
   Than your lips would ever say . . .

I thought I had forgotten,
   But it all came back again
Tonight with the first Spring thunder
   In a rush of rain.

Sara Teasdale

BREAKDOWN

THE alarm clock broke into his slumber,
   He rose up refreshed from his bed,
On a beautiful, sunny Spring morning —
   No sign of the trouble ahead.

He rode on his bike to the station,
   In time for the eight o'clock train.
He hummed as he strolled down the platform.
   (Let somebody else take the strain.)

The train arrived two minutes early,
   He easily managed a seat.
The crossword took less than ten minutes,
   And the coffee was hot, strong and sweet.

As soon as he entered the office
   He realised something was wrong.
His colleagues were huddled together,
   Their faces were worried and long.

"The power has gone out of the City,
   The computers have gone on the blink.
We might as well go home right now, sir,
   As there's nobody here who can think!"

Marion Elliot

BUTTERCUPS AND DAISIES

WHERE the dipping hawthorn dreams,
  Where the dimpling water streams,
Silver stars and golden moons
Buttercups and daisies.

Perfumed nosegays without names,
Dancing song and green-time games,
Weaving dreams and fairy chains
Of buttercups and daisies.

Here where Winter hides her face,
Deck the boughs with Summer lace,
Make the dell a fairy place
With buttercups and daisies!

Eileen Melrose

BY CARMARTHEN BAY

BEHOLD the happy three,
  Wading knee-deep through windy hyacinths
Against a beryl sea!

Dear wife, if only we
  Might hold them ever thus in idleness
Of April innocency!

Ah, no! Not so, not so!
  Rather 'tis our exceeding happiness
To watch our children grow —

Springing and burgeoning
  In the sweet light of Heaven, or, storm-beset,
Still bravely flourishing;

Gaining from Winter's stress
  No less than from the idle Summertide's
Full golden blessedness:

And as, in love with life,
  They swiftly grow to man and womanhood,
Even more ours, dear wife —

Even more surely ours
  Shall be their wise young hearts than when they played,
Flowerlike among the flowers:

While still, in memory,
  Three happy children among hyacinths,
Shall frolic by the sea.

Wilfrid Gibson

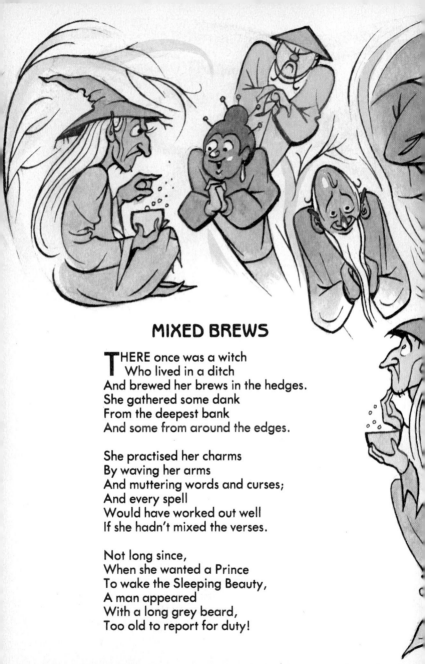

MIXED BREWS

THERE once was a witch
    Who lived in a ditch
And brewed her brews in the hedges.
She gathered some dank
From the deepest bank
And some from around the edges.

She practised her charms
By waving her arms
And muttering words and curses;
And every spell
Would have worked out well
If she hadn't mixed the verses.

Not long since,
When she wanted a Prince
To wake the Sleeping Beauty,
A man appeared
With a long grey beard,
Too old to report for duty!

When she hoped to save
Aladdin's cave
From his uncle cruel and cranky,
She concocted a spell
That somehow fell
Not on him, but on Widow Twankey.

With a magic bean
She called for a Queen
Who was locked in the wizard's castle.
There came an old hag
With a postman's bag
And threepence to pay on the parcel.

What comes of a witch
Who has hitch after hitch?
I'm afraid that there's no telling:
But I think, as a rule,
She returns to school
And tries to improve her spelling.

Clive Sansom

DOWN THE LANE

DOWN the lane is almond pink,
  Cherry white and tender green
Breaking on the hawthorn spray;
Daffdowndillies toss and preen,
Blown by North wind loud and keen,
Where the crocus from the clay
Points its yellow, mauve and blue,
And the snowdrop bows to you.
   Crocus, snowdrop, daffodil,
    Blue and mauve, white, yellow, green . . .
      Hush, the thrush:
   Time of year,
   March is here!

Down the lane high verdant slopes,
Shower-wet and sun-aglow,
Decked with hawthorn red and white,
Beds of pink-stained chestnut snow;
Pale laburnum left and right,
Lilac in the hedge below,
Scented privet, too, and one
Tall acacia in the sun;
And beyond, where lane slopes down,
Lime trees, beeches green and brown,
Sheltering the place where bees
Murmur in the apple trees.
   Hawthorn, beech, acacia,
    Rowan, chestnut, lilac, lime,
    Wallflower, pansy, iris . . .
      Hark! the lark:
   Time of year,
   May is here!

Shan Bullock

CHECK

THE night was creeping on the ground;
  She crept and did not make a sound
Until she reached the tree, and then
She covered it, and stole again
Along the grass beside the wall.

I heard the rustle of her shawl
As she threw blackness everywhere
Upon the sky and ground and air,
And in the room where I was hid:
But no matter what she did
To everything that was without,
She could not put my candle out.

So I stared at the night, and she
Stared back solemnly at me.

James Stephens

CANADIAN CAMPING SONG

A WHITE tent pitched by a glassy lake,
   Well under a shady tree,
Or by rippling rills from the grand old hills,
   Is the Summer home for me.
I fear no blaze of the noontide rays,
   For the woodland glades are mine,
The fragrant air, and that perfume rare
   The odour of forest pine.

A cooling plunge at the break of day,
   A paddle, a row, or sail,
With always a fish for a midday dish,
   And plenty of Adam's ale.
With rod or gun, or in hammock swung,
   We glide through the pleasant days;
When darkness falls on our canvas walls,
   We kindle the camp fire's blaze.

From out the gloom sails the silv'ry moon,
   O'er forests dark and still,
Now far, now near, ever sad and clear,
   Comes the plaint of the whippoorwill;
With song and laugh, and with kindly chaff,
   We startle the birds above,
Then rest tired heads on our cedar beds,
   To dream of the ones we love.

J. D. Edgar

PLYMOUTH

OH, what know they of harbours
   Who toss not on the sea?
They tell of fairer havens,
   But none so fair there be

As Plymouth town outstretching
   Her quiet arms to me,
Her breast's broad welcome spreading
   From Mewstone to Penlee.

And with this home-thought, darling,
   Come crowding thoughts of thee;
Oh! what know they of harbours
   Who toss not on the sea?

Ernest Radford

BLOSSOMTIME

I STOOD beneath a blossom tree,
  The sunshine on my face,
Like standing at an altar,
   An almost holy place,

The tiny petals falling
   Like a blessing from above,
Each wafting breeze a-blowing
   Soft winnowings of love;

The sweet shyness of bluebells,
   Was it fancy that they rang?
A tune of equal sweetness
   To the song the blackbird sang;

I was a bride of Maytime
   Alone beneath the tree,
And fancy held me spellbound
   At that altar just for me;

A primrose was my bouquet,
   The choir, the birds that sing,
I picked two tiny daisies
   To make my wedding ring,

Alas, who would I marry?
   Someone who smiles for me
With ways both sweet and gentle,
   To my heart I'd give the key.

                    Moyra Phyllis Crimp

THE WOOL WORK PICTURE

THE bright wool sun
 Shines on the green wool grass
Where the wool daisies grow,
And the wool glass
Of the white wool cottage window
Shows a row
Of wool geraniums,
And the gay wool flowers
In wool herbaceous borders
Bloom in eternal Summer
To light these Winter hours;
A black wool cat sits on
A brown wool chair,
And there is gold wool sunlight
Everywhere;
A picture made of wool
Long, long ago,
Yet on our wall it gives
The same warm glow
As when I was a child
And wished that I
Could run and play
Beneath the blue wool sky!

Aileen E. Passmore

A SONG

THE feathers of the willow
  Are half of them grown yellow
    Above the swelling stream;
And ragged are the bushes,
And rusty now the rushes,
    And wild the clouded gleam.

The thistle now is older,
His stalk begins to moulder,
    His head is white as snow;
The branches all are barer,
The linnet's song is rarer,
    The robin pipeth now.
                Richard Watson Dixon

SNOOZE MUSE

SITTING on a deck-chair in the garden — that's
   the life,
Free from situations where confusion may be rife.
Studying the busy bees on pollenating ploys,
And wishing that each butterfly would try to make
   less noise.

Sitting on a deck-chair in the garden — that's
   the kind
Of horticultural pursuit that fashions peace of mind.
Forgetting cares and worries, and then giving
   thoughts a prod
To take me on a journey to that Wonderland
   of Nod.

Sitting on a deck-chair in the garden — that's
   the scene,
Dreaming of a lawn that's rather like
   a bowling-green.
Where weeds are non-existent, and the toughest
   task perchance
Is listening to vibrations from gyrations by the ants.

Sitting on a deck-chair in the garden — that's
   for me,
Snoozing and refusing to be bothered by ennui.
I close my eyes, and analyse brave ventures
   to explore.
I'll put the world right, once again —
   I've done it all before.

J. M. Robertson

MISSED!

THE sun in the heavens was beaming:
  The breeze bore an odour of hay,
My flannels were spotless and gleaming,
  My heart was unclouded and gay;
The ladies, all gaily apparelled,
  Sat round looking on at the match,
In the tree-tops the dicky-birds carolled,
  All was peace till I bungled that catch.
My attention the magic of summer
  Had lured from the game — which was wrong;
The bee (that inveterate hummer)
  Was droning its favourite song.
I was tenderly dreaming of Clara
  (On her not a girl is a patch);
When, ah, horror! There soared through the air a
  Decidedly possible catch.
Oh ne'er, if I live to a million,
  Shall I feel such a terrible pang.
From the seats in the far-off pavilion
  A loud yell of ecstasy rang.
By the handful my hair (which is auburn)
  I tore with a wrench from my thatch,
And my heart was seared deep with a raw burn
  At the thought that I'd foozled that catch.
Ah, the bowler's low querulous mutter.
  Point's loud, unforgettable scoff!
Oh, give me my driver and putter!
  Henceforward my game shall be golf.
If I'm asked to play cricket hereafter,
  I am wholly determined to scratch.
Life's void of all pleasure and laughter;
  I bungled the easiest catch.

P. G. Wodehouse

WE'LL GO NO MORE A-ROVING

So, we'll go no more a-roving,
  So late into the night,
Though the heart be still as loving,
  And the moon be still as bright.

For the sword outwears its sheath,
  And the soul wears out the breast,
And the heart must pause to breathe,
  And love itself have rest.

Though the night was made for loving,
  And the day returns too soon,
Yet we'll go no more a-roving,
  By the light of the moon.

George Gordon, Lord Byron

BY THE SEASHORE

PLAGUED with the din of sects and factions,
  Sick of the greed that cries for more,
From pestering ills and vain distractions,
  I turn world-weary to the shore.

See the huge rollers rising greenly,
  Pile vast and slow their sun-shot wall,
Hang for a moment poised serenely,
  Then, wrecked, in thundering ruin fall.

Roaring they come, heaped-up and hoary,
  Smite the great rocks in bursts of spray,
Foam to my feet in surging glory,
  Then swirl their broken strength away.

Ah, heart, what matters joy or sorrow,
    Belief or doubt, oh, storm-tossed soul,
What vexed today or vague tomorrow,
    Here where the mighty waters roll?

Age upon age their voice goes booming,
    Leagues beyond leagues their wastes extend;
Deep calls to deep, whilst man, presuming,
    Wastes his vain heart on foe or friend.

Hate deep as hell or love supernal,
    Life's worst or best, seem here but spray
Tossed to the winds, where God's eternal
    Spills her long thunders night and day.

Lone as the desert Sphinx, more lonely,
    On lonelier wastes I gaze than he;
Deaf to all sounds but one sound only,
    The hoarse, wild mockery of the sea.

Latimer McInnes

MINISTERING ANGEL

YOU crashed about, then crept about,
   You rattled drawers and cupboard doo•
When I was ill.

You gave me scrambled eggs for tea,
What were those brown bits I could see?
I heard a thump, I heard you swear,
You dropped the butter on the stair
When I was ill.

You kicked the dog and chased the cat,
You searched and searched for this and that
So many things you couldn't find,
But you were good and oh, so kind
When I was ill!

Iris Hesselden

GRANNY'S ATTIC

UP in Granny's attic, there are lots and lots
   of things —
There's a great, big, china eagle, but it hasn't
   any wings.

There's a thing that's called a mangle — it was
   used, or so I'm told
To give the Monday wash a decent press in days of
   old.

There's a set of rusty golf-clubs Grandad used to
  win a cup;
There's a gramophone still working, but you have to
  wind it up.

There's a fairly fancy hat-box laid inside another
  case;
There's a jug without a handle, there's a clock
  without a face.

There's a picture of Great-Granny back in 1898;
A selection of sheet music in a rather sorry state.

There's a wireless from the Thirties, there's a fiddle
  with no strings.
The more I look around, the more I'm finding other
  things.

One day when I'm a Granny, my grandchildren may
  agree
The things in Granny's attic have a family history.

No matter what they find there, they will likely be
  emphatic,
"It's really quite amazing what's up there in
  Granny's attic."

J. M. Robertson

DOROTHY

DOROTHY is walking in the pleasant, daisied
   meadow,
   Young June incarnate in her pretty lilac gown;
Little breezes, playing, show a dainty silken
   stocking
   Peeping 'mong the ladysmocks and soft
   thistledown.

Dorothy is hasting up the fern-banked moorland
   highway,
   Mauve-winged butterfly, she goes floating lightly
   past,
Airy as the cotton-grass that June's sweet breath is
   blowing,
   Bright among the shadows that the dark rocks
   cast.

Dorothy is standing 'mid the fragrant, purpling
   heather,
   Poised like a flower in her pretty lilac gown,
Fresh as simple lavender that sweetens shady
   gardens,
   Dainty as the ladysmocks and silky thistledown.

Somebody is watching as she wanders thro' the
   meadow,
   Somebody is waiting as she flutters lightly past,
One who wants her fragrance to refresh life's lonely
   highway,
   Her brightness 'mong the shadows that the dark
   days cast.

Hylda C. Cole

CONSOLATION

O WINTER days are bleak and grey,
  And Winter nights are long:
No fireflies where the sedge grows,
No blossoms by the hedgerows,
And in the trees no song.

O Winter days, they end betimes,
The nights fall soon and deep:
Then hey for chair and fender-nook,
The pipe of peace with friend or book,
And long, dark hours of sleep.

Shan Bullock

A WISH

A LITTLE work, a little play,
  An endless sunshine holiday;
A little home beside the sea,
Ah, that's the life — the life for me!

I envy not the king his crown,
So I may range across the down,
Or, hidden in some shady nook,
Read still from Nature's story-book.

The winds may blow, the rains may fall,
I still shall hear the cuckoo call,
In shady woodlands deep withdrawn,
Or spy the blackbird on the lawn.

And if meanwhile the days go by
Devoid of pleasure, sullenly,
Still Nature smiles, though Life may frown,
Beneath the noisy whirl of town.

Tinsley Pratt

WILLOW WARBLER'S SONG

As April rain-drops, tremulously poised
   Upon a tree and shaken by the wind,
Scarcely fall but, air-borne, slide through sun
And shade, then gently slip and side-step down
The tender ladders of unfolding fern
To reach the pale, sun-dappled primrose discs;
And filter on in infinitesimal beads
Of silver freshness to renew the frail
And five-faced flowers of the moschatel;
Only to seep away, obliquely still,
Through lacy leaves, and lie at rest among
The lowly mosses that delight to throng
The moist and shadowed hollows of the ground;

So spills your little waterfall of sound
In brief, oblique, inconsequent cascade,
To shower down on all who hear you sing
The cool baptismal sweetness of the Spring.

Lilian Maude Watts

WELCOME

TIS sweet to hear the watch-dog's honest bark
  Bay deep-mouthed welcome as we draw
    near home,
'Tis sweet to know there is an eye will mark
Our coming, and look brighter when we come;
'Tis sweet to be awakened by the lark,
Or lulled by falling waters; sweet the hum
Of bees, the voice of girls, the song of birds,
The lisp of children, and their earliest words.

Lord Byron

THE WARNING

DON'T you walk down the twisty lane,
  Not when the twilight lingers,
Lest you hear the fairy folk's laughter plain,
  And be touched by their cool, soft fingers.

Never go there when the sunset glows,
  And the little, swift bats are flying,
Or you'll learn about things no wise child knows,
  And bitter will be your crying.

Keep to the house at the end of day,
  Or go when I'm there beside you;
Lest the fairyland dancers steal you away,
  And deep in a dream they'll hide you.

Peter Cliffe

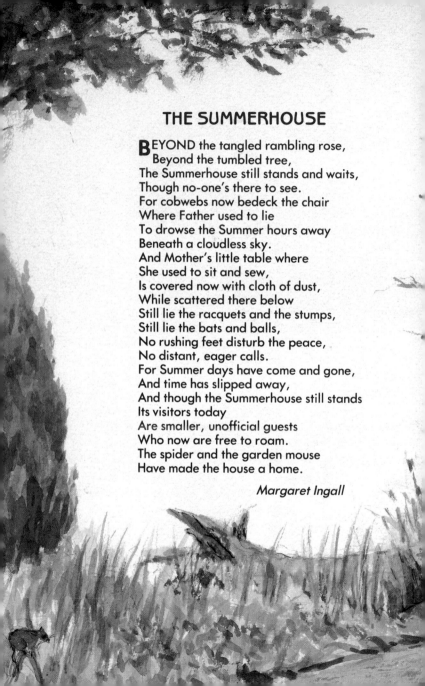

THE SUMMERHOUSE

BEYOND the tangled rambling rose,
  Beyond the tumbled tree,
The Summerhouse still stands and waits,
Though no-one's there to see.
For cobwebs now bedeck the chair
Where Father used to lie
To drowse the Summer hours away
Beneath a cloudless sky.
And Mother's little table where
She used to sit and sew,
Is covered now with cloth of dust,
While scattered there below
Still lie the racquets and the stumps,
Still lie the bats and balls,
No rushing feet disturb the peace,
No distant, eager calls.
For Summer days have come and gone,
And time has slipped away,
And though the Summerhouse still stands
Its visitors today
Are smaller, unofficial guests
Who now are free to roam.
The spider and the garden mouse
Have made the house a home.

Margaret Ingall

HIGH SUMMER

SHIMMER of sunbeams on bright water,
   Glimmer of daisies, scent of hay,
Church bells chiming — oh, so softly,
   Over the fields, from far away.
Dabble of ducklings on the river,
   Downy and golden, drifting by,
Willows, with pale green, tossing tresses,
   Under the bluest-ever sky.
Murmur of wild doves in the coppice,
   Laughter of children at their play,
Oh, this is Summer in all its glory,
   This is a perfect Summer's day!

Kathleen O'Farrell

FELL WALKING SONG

WHEN city days are dark and drear
    Or trouble sounds a warning bell,
I send my thoughts, for just a while,
    To windswept hill, high rolling fell;
Beyond the line of climbing trees,
    Beyond the fields in Summer dress,
To where the crags reach through the clouds,
    And there is joyful emptiness.

And when at last my work is done,
   And mundane problems cast aside,
I follow where my thoughts have led,
   Anticipation as my guide.
I hear the music of the wind,
   I hear the wild song of the birds,
No idle conversation here,
   Enchantment has no need of words.

Though Autumn storms and Springtime rain
   Send drifting clouds across the peaks,
I gather beauty just the same
   To combat worry through the weeks.
I store the magic in my heart,
   Until my feet take me once more
Along the path, beyond the trees,
   To where my thoughts have gone before.

Iris Hesselden

THE COTTAGE

NOBLY and well 'twas said — true wealth alone
    Resides with him who best can do without!
So, while I sIt on this heath-cushioned stone,
I harbour in my heart no vexing doubt
Whether, or no, the vain world with its shows
Is worthy of a wise man's grave concern:
Here the sun shines, the fragrant south wind blows,
And Nature's open pages bid me learn
All that brings peace, and joy, and rich content:
My little lodge, fair-seeming, offers me
The food and medicine of the soul, well-blent,
And fills me with a proud philosophy—
Knowing right well this cottage on the moor
Holds that which makes a millionaire seem poor.

John Hogben

ARMCHAIR TRAVELLER

I SIT in my chair and I just close my eyes,
    And I travel so far and so wide.
I see a clear sky and a small Cornish cove
    And I wait for the turn of the tide.
Then when the wind blows in the chimney at night
    And the gusts turn loudly to gales,
I close my eyes tighter and then I'm away,
    And I'm free on the green Yorkshire dales.
Sometimes when the rain pit-a-pats on the glass,
    Then I'm off to the Highlands and back,
I sail on the lochs and climb the high hills
    And there's nothing at all that I lack.

I sit in the dusk when lights twinkle outside,
    And the world is so quiet and still.
I travel to Grasmere and walk by the lake,
    And I'm joyful with each daffodil.
I sit by the fire when the weather is cold,
    And the forecast is snow everywhere,
I just close my eyes, and it's Summer once more
    As I travel again in my chair.

Iris Hesselden

SUGGESTION

A GARDEN is maybe the perfect place
    To be in Summertime,
No need for tiring, lengthy chase
    To some distant clime.

A spreading tree, a fresh-mown lawn,
    A few fragrant flowers,
A deck chair to recline upon,
    And a book to pass the hours.

Dorothy Anderson

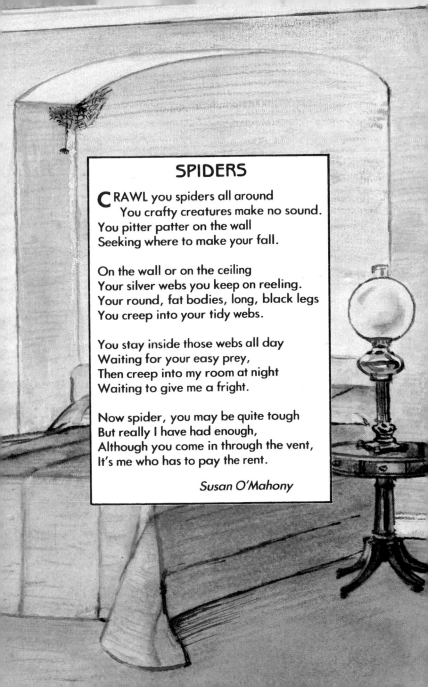

SPIDERS

CRAWL you spiders all around
    You crafty creatures make no sound.
You pitter patter on the wall
Seeking where to make your fall.

On the wall or on the ceiling
Your silver webs you keep on reeling.
Your round, fat bodies, long, black legs
You creep into your tidy webs.

You stay inside those webs all day
Waiting for your easy prey,
Then creep into my room at night
Waiting to give me a fright.

Now spider, you may be quite tough
But really I have had enough,
Although you come in through the vent,
It's me who has to pay the rent.

Susan O'Mahony

THE SHELL

I THOUGHT of what might lie ahead,
   The downward path, once youth had fled,
The meaning of life — of Heaven and Hell,
You smiled — and handed me a shell.

You raced the waves with easy grace,
The sun caressed your open face,
Your hair uplifted, shone, wind-tossed,
You laughed and said, "Don't count the cost.
Don't worry o'er life's treasures — live,
Don't hoard life's gifts and treasures — give.
Those restless waves that ebb and flow,
They do not ask which way to go."

I walked beside you, shell in hand,
You wrote your name upon the sand,
The sky so bright turned cold and grey,
Life's waves had washed your name away.
I walked alone throughout the years,
Your memory still evokes my tears,
Your love of life, and its bright flame,
Bring me to where you wrote your name.

I pick a shell from off the sand,
And hold it softly in my hand.
My heart, it still remembers well,
You smiled — and handed me a shell.

                    William Mackay

ROSES IN THE RAIN

SUNSHINE has made my garden plot
   Arid and very bare;
Too many days, all stifling hot,
   Have left their impress there.

But now the rain is falling fast
   On rose, and bush and tree,
And all is fresh and green at last,
   And clothed in fragrancy.

So, when my heart is barren — dry —
   As my hard garden plot,
May showers be sent in sweet supply,
   Though I deserve them not.

Let all my senses be set free
   From worry, fret and strain,
Help me to feel love cleansing me,
   As roses in the rain.

Margaret H. Dixon.

REQUEST

L EAVE me not in the churchyard
　　When I am laid to rest,
But bear me up to the lonely hills
　　That look towards the west.

Give me the heath for cover,
　　A slab of the mountain stone;
Give me the song of the restless wind,
　　And leave me there, alone.

Give me the far horizon
　　Of sea, and the open sky,
With winds that rustle the sunlit heath
　　And shadows passing by.

Give me the dawn and sunset,
　　And leave my spirit free
To ride alone on the changeless hills,
　　Where it will always be.

Iris M. Raikes

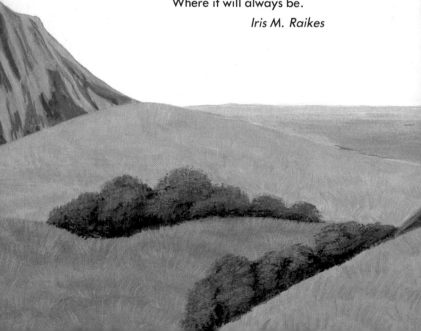

RIVER SONG

NO music save the wild bird's cry,
No canopy but grey-blue sky.
No wine to dull or cloud the eye,
No clock to tell how time slips by.
Just peace along the river.

No traffic noise assails the ear,
No siren sound, arousing fear.
No shouting voice, no jibe nor jeer,
No cause for worry, doubt or tear.
Just peace along the river.

No hostile thoughts of hurt or spite,
No happier sound, no sweeter sight.
No calmer scene in evening light,
No better place for true delight.
Just peace beside the river.

Iris Hesselden

A MEMORY

THIS I remember,
 I cannot tell why,
A Cambridgeshire fen,
And a jade-coloured sky;
Wild geese that flew
Just as daylight was done,
White feathers gold-tipped
By the fast-fading sun;
A pale heron perched
On the bank of the dyke,
Patiently, hopefully,
Waiting for pike;
A horse plodding homeward,
An old ruined mill,
An uncanny feeling
Of time standing still.

It's framed in my memory,
I wish I knew why,
The silence, the stillness,
The jade-coloured sky . . .

Kathleen O'Farrell

AS WINTER COMES

THERE are three smells that I shall always love,
   Being country bred —
The smell of burning weeds
At the ditch-back in white October when
The winds are frosty, and cheery voices of men
And children's laughter carry far across
The fields, and the great billows of smoke
Roll down and out and blow over the sky.

The smell of bracken and whins burning at dusk
When greedy, licking tongues of yellow flame
Leap in the air, and the long, solemn slopes
Close in, watchful and silent, till the world
Is full of eeriness, and shadowy things
Crowd jostling round.

But best of all I love
The heavy, bitter taste of peatfire smoke
Sharp in the eyes and raw to city throats;
Clinging to tweeds and corners, pungent, strong,
The tang of farms and mountains, country things
In Winter when the bogs gleam silver and black:
The reek o' Kings! the incense of the land:
Ireland's own perfume, and the smell of home.

Sydney Bell

NOVEMBER

MISTY, mournful, dripping, sodden,
   Surely no reward is here?
Leafless woodlands rarely trodden,
   Muddy roads a dreary smear.

Vision-dimming fogs descending,
   Clouds a melancholy pall;
Midday sun with lamplight blending,
   Darkness ere the night can fall.

That's November. Who'll commend it,
   Champion its sullen airs?
Ask the children: they'll defend it.
   Guy Fawkes marked the month as theirs.

Bonfires blazing . . . rockets jetting . . .
   Catherine wheels in fiery flower.
Brief and brilliant, in the darkness,
   That's November's finest hour!

Noel Scott

THE PEBBLE

THIS pebble that I picked so idly from the shore,
  Glistening, damp, polished with the coming
And going of the tide; see how many colours
Are prisoned there! A prism, if you look into it
  closely.
Yet, if I hold it at a distance from my eyes,
It is one with this beach of rusted terracotta.
And the sea, which threw it up into my hand,
That too is filled with many colours,
So many ripples riding towards the shore.

The stone dissolves; the sea and all its tumult
Fades: the sand, the sunlight and the cries of mews.
There is nothing or everything: what you see there,
Emptiness or creation: what you hear there,
Endless silence or the turbulent mystery of the wind.

Bryan Cave-Browne-Cave

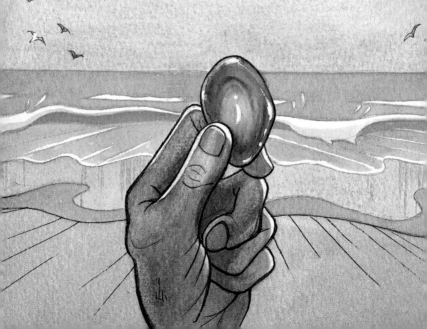

The artists are:—

Charles Bannerman; Breakdown, Blossomtime, Missed!, Fell Walking Song, Suggestion, Spiders, The Shell, As Winter Comes.

Sheila Carmichael; The Laggard, Spring Song, A Song, The Summerhouse, The Cottage, Roses In The Rain, River Song.

John Dugan; Ministering Angel, Armchair Traveller.

Barbara Glebska; The Warning, Request.

Allan Haldane; Canadian Camping Song, Consolation.

Harry McGregor; The Stripling Thames, Down The Lane, By The Seashore.

John Mackay; The Call, No Easy Way, Thoughts From The City, Mixed Brews, Check, Plymouth, The Wool Work Picture, A Wish, The Pebble.

Norma Maclean; Grey Eyes, April Love, Buttercups And Daisies, Dorothy.

Sandy Milligan; Blue Of The Bluebells, Spring Rain, Snooze Muse, Welcome.

Douglas Phillips; By Carmarthen Bay.

Staff Artists; The Answer, We'll Go No More A-Roving, Granny's Attic, Willow Warbler's Song, A Memory, The Visionary, November.

THE VISIONARY

SILENT is the house: all are laid asleep:
  One alone looks out o'er the snow-wreaths
    deep,
Watching every cloud, dreading every breeze
That whirls the wildering drift, and bends the
    groaning trees.

Cheerful is the hearth, soft the matted floor;
Not one shivering gust creeps through pane or
    door;
The little lamp burns straight, its rays shoot strong
    and far:
I trim it well, to be the wanderer's guiding-star.

Frown, my haughty sire! chide, my angry dame!
Set your slaves to spy; threaten me with shame:
But neither sire nor dame nor prying serf shall know
What angel nightly tracks that waste of frozen
    snow.

What I love shall come like visitant of air,
Safe in secret power from lurking human snare;
What loves me, no word of mine shall e'er betray,
Though for faith unstained my life must forfeit pay.

Burn, then, little lamp; glimmer straight and
    clear—
Hush! a rustling wing stirs, methinks, the air:
He for whom I wait, thus ever comes to me;
Strange Power! I trust thy might; trust thou my
    constancy.

Emily Bronte